WONDER WOMEN

HEROINES OF HISTORY

IDA B. WELLS

NICOLE K.
ORR

PURPLE TOAD
PUBLISHING

Printing   1   2   3   4   5   6   7   8   9

PUBLISHER'S NOTE
This series, Wonder Women: Heroines of History, covers racism and misogyny in United States history. Some of the events told in this series may be disturbing to young readers. The first-person narrative in chapter one of this book is a work of fiction based on the author's research.

Ida B. Wells
Nellie Bly
Sacagawea
Stagecoach Mary
Sybil Ludington

Library of Congress Cataloging-in-Publication Data
Orr, Nicole K.
  Ida Wells / Written by Nicole K. Orr.
     p. cm.
Includes bibliographic references, glossary, and index.
ISBN 9781624694431
1. Ida B. Wells. 1862 - 1931 — Juvenile literature. 2. African American women civil rights — Biography — Juvenile literature. 3. Civil rights movements — United States — History — Juvenile literature. I. Series: Wonder Women
 E185.97.W55 A45 2019
 323/.092 B
[B]

eBook ISBN: 9781624694424

Library of Congress Control Number: 2018943946

ABOUT THE AUTHOR: Nicole K. Orr has been writing for as long as she's known how to hold a pen. She is the author of several other books by Purple Toad Publishing and has won National Novel Writing Month eleven times. Orr lives in Portland, Oregon, and camps under the stars whenever she can. When she isn't writing, she's traveling the world or taking road trips.

CONTENTS

TREATING HER LIKE A LADY

CHAPTER ONE

When I boarded the train in Memphis, Tennessee, I didn't know my whole life was about to change. It was September 15, 1883, and nearly 3:30 in the afternoon.

I waited on the platform belonging to the Chesapeake and Ohio Railroad Company as the train pulled into the station. There were two cars for holding people and one car for holding their bags. When the cars were no longer moving, I got onto the front one. I saw a man stumble down the aisle. As I walked by him, the smell of alcohol was overwhelming. I held my breath as I hurried out of the crowded car and into the next one. There were people in this car too. They looked at me as I came in and then looked away just as quickly. Their skin was a different color than mine, but I still felt safer with them than I had with the drunk white man. I

A train station in the 1880s in Memphis, Tennessee. Ida B. Wells wasn't the only one to feel unsafe boarding or disembarking from a train. Many African Americans of the time were nervous to travel by rail because, if trouble broke out, it was hard to get help.

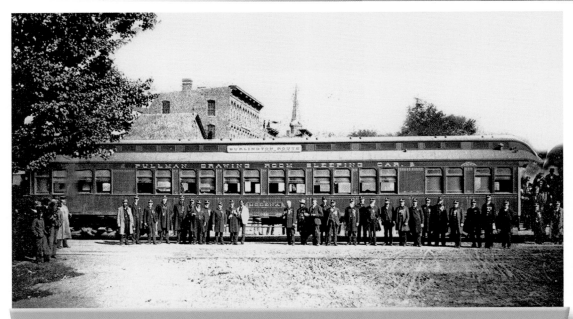

The late 1880s was a very exciting time for railroad companies. People were discovering that train travel was affordable and could provide transportation for those who didn't own cars. The rides, however, weren't always comfortable and breakdowns were common.

did not like riding in the forward car. People who smoked and drank sat in that coach.

I found a seat on the rear coach. As I waited for the train to start moving, I planned what I'd teach when I got back to school. It is a wonderful thing to love what you do for a living. Some women were born to be mothers. Some were born to be wives or nurses. I'd been born to be a teacher, and there were few things in my life that made me happier.

The train soon began moving. I opened the newspaper I'd brought with me and enjoyed having the two seats to myself.

"Your ticket, ma'am?" a voice asked me.

"Of course!" I folded my newspaper and put it in my lap. I pulled out my ticket and smiled at the conductor. The moment he saw the color of my face, he frowned.

"I cannot accept this ticket in this car," he said, and then continued walking.

For a moment, I was so surprised and so confused, I didn't do anything at all. I looked very closely at my ticket. Why would he not accept it? What had I done wrong?

I was still staring at the small piece of paper when the conductor came back. When he did not want to see my ticket, I knew the problem wasn't to do with the paper, but to do with me.

"You are in the wrong car, ma'am." His voice was so gentle, it seemed he thought I was there by accident. "Would you please move to the front coach?" he asked.

"No." I shook my head. "The front car is very crowded. I have ridden in it before. The men in there smoke and are drunk. I would like to stay here."

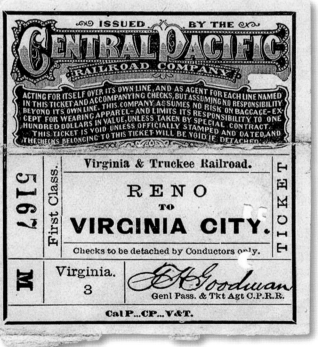

Train tickets like this one from 1878 were printed on card stock, making it easier for the ticket punch to cut out particular shapes.

"This car is for people like me." He pointed at the color of his face. "The front car is for people like you. Please move to the other car."

I must have misunderstood him. This went against the Civil Rights Act of 1875! The Civil Rights Act was supposed to keep people of color from being thrown out of public spaces such as hotels, theaters, restaurants, and railroad cars.

"You cannot make me leave," I explained very reasonably. "I know my rights. I have seen colored people ride in both cars. I have a seat right here and I intend to keep it."

James Rapier of Alabama was one of seven African American representatives who helped pass the Civil Rights Act of 1875. The act outlawed discrimination on trains and in restaurants.

"I am trying to treat you like a lady," he began, but I cut him off.

"If you were to treat me like a lady, you would leave me alone."

When he finally walked away, I sighed with relief. I was 20 years old, but white men could still scare me. It hurt, too, when I glanced around at the other people in the car and saw the looks on their faces. How could they be scared of me? I hadn't done anything wrong!

When we were pulling into the train station at Fraziers, the conductor returned. I sighed. When the

Around the time Wells refused to give up her first-class seat on the train, the U.S. Supreme Court declared the Civil Rights Act of 1875 unconstitutional. Public places, including public restrooms, rail cars, hotels, and dance clubs, again became segregated. They would remain so until the Civil Rights Act of 1964.

Civil Rights Act had been passed, I'd thought my days of being discriminated against were over. Apparently I'd been wrong.

"I will not move to the other car," I told him before he'd even opened his mouth. "I am a school teacher. I bought a ticket just like all of these nice folks." I waved an arm at the other passengers. The train had stopped. They were all watching us. "You cannot make me leave because I am a colored woman."

"You will move." The man took hold of my arm with a dangerous shine in his eyes. "If you do not, I will stop treating you like a lady."

"When did you start?" I barely had the time to get the words out before he attempted to drag me from where I sat. I would not let him. I held on to my seat and I did not let go.

"Help me!" the conductor shouted, and two white men joined him in his efforts. Together, the three finally forced me out of my seat.

"Do not do this!" I yelled as I was picked up in their arms. I struggled as my newspaper fell to the floor under the men's feet. The sleeve of my shirt ripped. I kicked and fought as I was carried to the platform between the two passenger cars. I grew desperate enough to bite the hand that held me. The conductor immediately let me go. Instead of giving in and walking into the next coach, I got off the train.

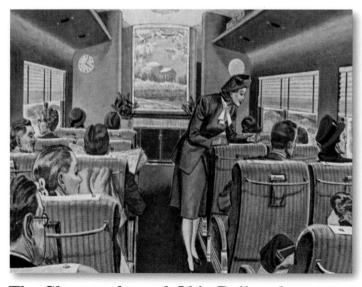

The Chesapeake and Ohio Railroad continued to promote whites-only ridership, as this ad from the 1940s shows.

"You do not need to leave the train!" the conductor called out to me as I marched away from him.

"I teach children, sir," I responded over my shoulder, refusing to turn back to him. "I should hope I do a better job of teaching them how to treat ladies than your teacher taught you!"[1]

CIVIL RIGHTS ACTIVIST ROSA PARKS

Seventy-two years after Ida B. Wells refused to give up her seat on a train, Rosa Parks refused to give up her seat on a bus. Born in 1913, Parks lived in Montgomery, Alabama. She spent most of her life fighting for civil rights. During her lifetime, the races were supposedly considered equal, but they were still required to lead separate lives. Whites and blacks had separate churches, schools, restaurants, waiting rooms, and even bathrooms.

Rosa Parks experienced these segregation laws every day of her life, but the day she took a stand was December 1, 1955. She had just boarded a bus home from work, and sat in a seat near the front. She was supposed to take a seat in the back, since those in the front were for white people. Soon enough, white men boarded and Parks was asked to move to the back. When she refused, she was arrested for breaking the laws of segregation.

The African-Americans living in Montgomery were angry, and many agreed not to use the buses until the law was changed. The Montgomery Bus Boycott lasted 381 days. When Parks went to trial, the court decided that the segregation laws were wrong. It was unclear at the time whether this happened because the laws were wrong or because the Montgomery bus line couldn't run anymore if black people stopped using it. Either way, Rosa Parks became known as "the mother of the civil rights movement."[2]

Rosa Parks

11

When Ida B. Wells was born on July 16, 1862, the United States was at war. The country had been debating the importance of slavery for years. People in some parts of the country felt slavery was good for business, and it was just a part of life. Others thought owning people as property was wrong. When Abraham Lincoln was voted president, the southern states panicked. Lincoln did not approve of slavery. The southern states thought that Lincoln would outlaw slavery. In response, 11 states in the South declared they would no longer be part of the United States. They split off and called themselves the Confederate States of America. Civil War officially began in 1861, partly because neither side could agree on how to handle slavery. The battle was bloody and long, and it was during this time that Ida B. Wells' parents met.

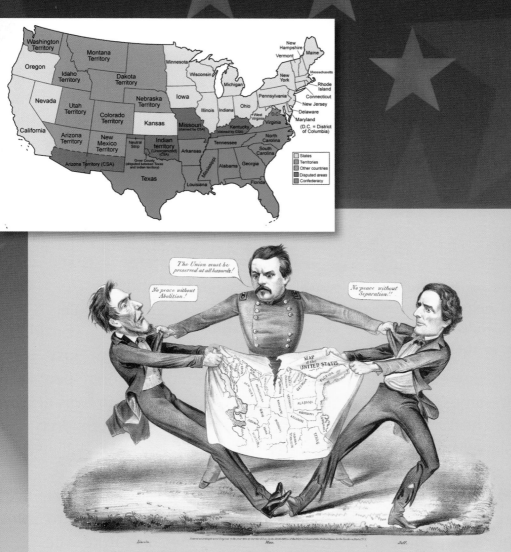

THE TRUE ISSUE OR "THATS WHATS THE MATTER".

Slavery was such a heated topic, it divided communities, families, marriages, and even friendships. To tell the world about this conflict, newspapers released cartoons such as this one where U.S. President Lincoln and Confederate President Jefferson Davis nearly tear a map of the United States in two.

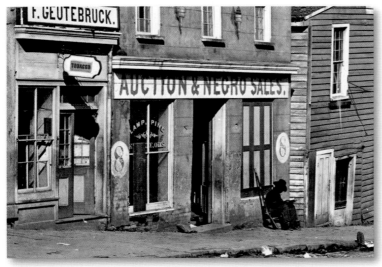

A slave trader shop in the south, 1864. People would inspect the person they were buying. They would ask to see the slave's teeth and listen to them speak.

James Wells and Elizabeth Warrenton met in Holly Springs, Mississippi. This was a very dangerous place for African Americans. Mississippi was one of the 11 southern states that were fighting to keep slavery legal. Slaves were considered property. Just as a person owned a house or livestock, he could also own people as slaves. James Wells was a slave. The man who owned him was also his father. The slave owner was permitted by law to have children with the slaves he owned. James' African American mother, Polly, was a slave owned by his father.

Most slaves were bought and sold multiple times in their lives. James only ever had one master. His father apprenticed him to Spires Bolling, a carpenter. It was there that James met his future wife.

Elizabeth Warrenton also lived in bondage. Born in 1884, she had been bought and sold many, many times. When she met James, she was owned by Bolling. Elizabeth was a cook in his household when an almost 19-year-old James Wells walked in. They fell in love, but because of the laws of Mississippi, they were not allowed to marry.

The couple stayed in Holly Springs and continued serving Bolling. During the war, the city changed hands more than 52 times. Sometimes the Confederate Army would take control of the city. Then the Union Army would take it back. Masters were constantly terrified that they were going to lose their slaves. Slaves were never sure if their freedom was near or years away. During this chaos, James and Elizabeth started a family. Their first child was Ida Bell.

Ida was only six months old when President Abraham Lincoln passed an order called the Emancipation Proclamation. Beginning January 1, 1863, the order stated, slaves living in the Confederate States could no longer be "owned" by anyone. They were free!

At first, the order created confusion. The Confederacy didn't believe they had to follow the law of the U.S. president, but the people in bondage believed their chains were legally broken. Some slaves fled the South. Those who stayed were overwhelmed with extra work. Union and Confederate soldiers alike would find slaves who had been

The Emancipation Proclamation is considered one of President Abraham Lincoln's greatest achievements.

General Robert E. Lee surrenders to General Grant (left) after the final battle of the war.

freed by the proclamation. The soldiers wouldn't know whether to arrest them or let them go.

The Civil War ended in 1865. The northern and southern states came back together as the United States of America. There was, however, just as much confusion as there had been before. Former slaves and owners didn't know where they stood with each other. Owners still had jobs that needed doing—but now they would have to pay their workers.

There were more than 450,000 newly freed slaves in the state of Mississippi who needed to earn a living. In the end, many slaves went back to the same households they had been in before. James Wells was one of them. Once the war was over, Spires Bolling asked James to work for him. James accepted the job.

Now that they were free, James and Elizabeth were finally allowed to marry. They could also send their children to school. (They would have a total of four sons and four daughters.) Ida went to so many schools as a child, she later would not be able to remember them all. She would not even be able to remember where she went first or last. As she explained, "Our job was to go to school and learn all we could."[1] She loved reading almost more than anything else. Books taught her about the world, about politics, and about the Civil War—but they did not teach her about people like her. "I had read the Bible and Shakespeare through, but I had never read a Negro book or anything about Negros," she later explained in her biography.[2]

This realization would change her life and the lives of thousands of others.

A BELOVED AMERICAN PRESIDENT

During his life and after his death, Abraham Lincoln was considered one of the most loved presidents in American history. He was born on February 12, 1809, to a family that had very little money. Their home only had three walls, so they made a fire where the fourth wall would have been to keep the cold out. There wasn't enough money to send Abraham to more than one year of school. Instead, he taught himself through books. He would sometimes walk for hours to the houses of neighbors in search of new books to read.

Lincoln, who preferred to be called Abe, held several different jobs before he was president. These included woodcutter, shopkeeper, general store owner, soldier, and lawyer. When he was 25, he entered politics for the first time and was voted into the Illinois State Senate. In 1860, he became president.

Many people did not believe he would be a good leader. He had come from a poor family and poor schooling. Lincoln won people's respect by being charming and kind. When he wanted people's attention, he went out to their farms and their homes to meet them personally. He treated all people equally. By the time he was killed on April 14, 1865, he was much loved. The nation missed him deeply.

Abraham Lincoln

In 1878, yellow fever swept through Holly Springs. Ida survived, but lost both her parents and one of her siblings. These deaths changed her life dramaticallly. She was 16 years old and just finishing high school. When her parents died, her siblings were to be separated into different homes. She refused to let that happen. Ida got a teaching job six miles from where she lived with her remaining family. In order to become a teacher, she pretended to be 18.

Her routine was not easy. She explained, "I came home every Friday afternoon, riding the six miles on the back of a big mule. I spent Saturday and Sunday washing and ironing and cooking for the children and went back to my country school on Sunday afternoon."[1]

Around 1880, Ida began attending classes at Fisk University in Nashville, Tennessee. It was also during this time that Ida's family began to spread out. One

Yellow fever is spread by female mosquitoes. Its name comes from the color it turns an infected person's skin, and from the deadly high fever it causes.

of her sisters, Eugenia, went to live with relatives. Two of Ida's brothers, Jim and George, were old enough to become apprentices to carpenters. Ida and her other sisters, Annie and Lily, moved in with their aunt Fannie Wells in Memphis, Tennessee. There, Ida's teaching career and her future as an activist took a huge leap forward. After she was dragged out of her seat on the train from Memphis to Nashville, Tennessee, she was determined to do more for civil rights.

The Chesapeake and Ohio Railroad was a powerful company that used its own magazine for years to enhance its image.

What happened to Wells on the train was not uncommon. Black people were often kept separate from white people. Laws were passed to change this, but many railroad companies, hotels, and restaurants continued to follow Jim Crow—to keep the races separate. When Wells was told to change railroad coaches, it made her angry enough to do something about it. She sued the Chesapeake and Ohio Railroad Company. While the circuit court awarded her $500, the decision was later overturned. She was upset by how she and her case had been handled. She knew others had to have been treated worse and wanted to reach out to them, so she wrote articles on race and politics. One of her first pieces was published in *The Living Way Magazine*. It was called "Iola."[2]

The name Iola began showing up more and more as the years went by. Wells began writing for the magazine *Free Speech and Headlight*. Eventually she purchased partial ownership of the magazine. In 1887, she went to the National African-American Press Convention.

Wells's growing fame sometimes brought hardship. In 1891, she was teaching at a public school where the students were almost entirely white. The school fired her because of her strong opinions about race and how blacks were treated in public schools. The topic of racism was dangerous, regardless of whether one was talking to a white person or a black person. Either way, those who promoted equal rights were often beaten or killed.

In 1892, Ida's friend Thomas Moss lost his life after a racial battle. He and two other black men owned the People's Grocery in Memphis. The store was making a lot of money. Across the street was another grocery store, this one owned by white men. These men were jealous of how popular the People's Grocery was and believed that store was stealing their customers. On March 9, 1892, the white men attacked the

A marker stands on the former site of the People's Grocery, at the junction of Walker Avenue and Mississippi Boulevard.

People's Grocery. The white men were injured, and the black men were arrested for the attack. There was no trial. The black men were taken from the Memphis jail and put to death.

When Wells heard about the lynching of Moss and his business partners, she was angry. One of the first things she did was write the booklet *Southern Horrors: Lynch Law in All Its Phases*. It covered the history of racism and lynching. The booklet so enraged the people of Memphis, they destroyed the *Free Speech* offices. They even threatened Ida's life. Wells was even more upset. She was trying to save the lives of African Americans living in Memphis. Instead, the white population was trying to chase her out of the city.

To stay safe, Wells moved to New York—but she kept fighting. Armed with her anger, she toured through the United States and then overseas to the United Kingdom. She believed very deeply that if people knew what was happening to black people in America, people everywhere would help stop it. She made it her mission to tell the world.

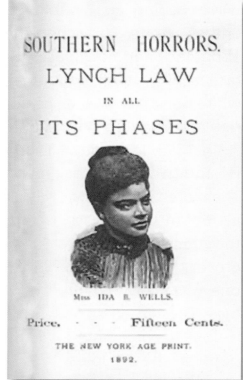

Southern Horrors angered racists, who then attacked and destroyed the offices of Free Speech.

LYNCHING STATISTICS

In the United States, the Constitution guarantees its citizens the right to a fair trial. But after the Civil War and well into the 1960s, it was not uncommon for people to be arrested, jailed, and then dragged out and killed before they ever stood trial.

The National Association for the Advancement of Colored People (NAACP) did several studies on just how widespread lynching was during this time period. According to these studies, between 1882 and 1968, there were 4,743 lynchings in the United States. Of those, 3,446 victims were black. The remaining 1,297 people were white, but there were still racist reasons for their murders. They tended to be friends of black people or they spoke out against the unfair treatment of blacks. In Ida B. Wells's home state of Mississippi, 581 people were lynched during those 86 years.[3]

A woman begs her president to help end racial violence in this cartoon.

THE PRINCESS OF THE PRESS

When she was young, Ida B. Wells had to focus on the safety and survival of her family. With adulthood, she had the opportunity to send her message into the world. In little time at all, the world began calling Ida B. Wells the Princess of the Press.

Wells went on tour twice in order to spread her message as far as she could. The first tour began in the wake of her friends' being lynched in 1892. She started with the states and then went to the United Kingdom. She heard countless stories of being lynched. She told others the ugly reality of what lynching was. The trip was risky. As Margaret Truman described in her book *Women of Courage*, "To call this dangerous work is an understatement. Imagine a lone black woman in some small town in Alabama or Mississippi, asking questions that no man wanted to answer about a crime that half the whites in the town had committed."[1]

Ida B. Wells spoke up for African Americans in a country that was quick to lynch them. She fought for the rights of women in a time when women were not considered equal to men. She was outspoken and brave, and she proved what women could be if they fought for it.

Her second tour was in 1893. Wells was invited to Great Britain by an activist named Catherine Impey. While she was there, Wells gave lectures on race, politics, and human rights. She took advantage of every opportunity to speak or to have her words printed. With each speech she gave, Wells gained fans and enemies. Her fans thought of her as a hero. Her enemies sent her threats and called her names. For protection, Wells bought a gun.

After she finished giving lectures across the country and abroad, Wells settled down in Illinois. She began writing for Chicago's first black newspaper, the *Chicago Conservator*. It was around this time that she began working with activist Frederick Douglass. He had also been born a slave, and he had spent much of his life trying to end slavery. When Wells heard that African Americans were not allowed to participate in the upcoming 1893 World's Columbian Exposition, she contacted Douglass. Wells and Douglass got together with Wells' partner at the *Chicago Conservator*, Ferdinand Lee Barnett. The three of them wrote a booklet titled *The Reason Why the Colored American Is Not Represented in the World's Columbian Exposition*. More than 10,000 copies were given out at

Frederick Douglass was very important to the Civil Rights Movement.

the fair. They helped raise awareness of the issues that Wells was so valiantly fighting for.

Wells released her first book, *A Red Record*, in 1895. In it were some of the interviews she had done on lynching. Hoping to reach as many white readers as possible, she included interviews only with white people. This was one of her riskiest writings. She included the names, dates, and locations of people who were lynched. She even included photographs. *A Red Record* made people uncomfortable and made it impossible for them to stay blind to the reality of lynching. This was, of course, exactly what Wells wanted.

Ferdinand Lee Barnett and Ida B. Wells shared a passion in promoting civil rights. He is especially remembered for his 1879 speech, "Race Unity."

The same year she released her first book, Wells fell in love with her partner at the *Chicago Conservator*, Ferdinand Lee Barnett. The two were married on June 27. Wells changed her last name to Wells-Barnett. The couple would have four children.

Wells-Barnett spent the rest of her life writing books, newspapers, and articles. She started the National Association for Colored Women in 1896. She gave lectures, raised money, and grew passionate about

The National Afro-American Council played a vital role in the civil rights movement. Its many members included Wells (front row, fourth from right) and Booker T. Washington. (front row, seconnd from left).

women's suffrage. At the time, women were not allowed to vote in elections.

In 1898, Wells-Barnett went to the White House in Washington, D.C. She demanded that President William McKinley stop lynching around the country, or at least to change the laws that protected it. She said of lynching, "I am only a mouthpiece through which to tell the story of lynching and I have told it so often that I know it by heart. I do not have to embellish; it makes its own way."[2] She made a second trip to the White House in 1913 as a member of the National Equal Rights League.

One of the largest organizations Wells was involved with was the National Association for the Advancement of Colored People (NAACP). She joined around 1909, but didn't stay long. Always a person of strong actions and intense opinions, Wells did not feel the NAACP was making enough progress. Today, Ida B. Wells-Barnett is considered one of the founding members of the NAACP.

Another organization Wells helped create was the Negro Fellowship League (NFL) in 1910. The center began as a reading room and gathering place for blacks in Chicago. Soon, it grew into a place where blacks who had recently moved to Chicago could receive food, shelter, and help finding jobs. Another goal of the NFL was to fight racial injustice in the criminal system. She and Ferdinand, who was an attorney, aided prisoners who were falsely accused of crimes or who were given harsher sentences than the crime warranted.

Three years later, she started the Alpha Suffrage Group. She also founded the first club for African American women in Chicago. Called the Ida B. Wells Club, it established a kindergarten for black children.

Nearing the end of her life, Wells did not slow down. The last two things she did were big and certainly left their mark on the history books.

In a time when women were fighting for their right to vote, you might think all women would fight together. This rarely happened. While black women and white women were fighting for the same thing, they fought for it separately. Ida B. Wells led the way for African American women. Susan B. Anthony led the

Susan B. Anthony was once arrested for voting in a presidential election. It was 1872 and she was fined $100. She refused to pay.

Alice Paul

way for white women. The two groups respected each other and sometimes even inspired each other, but they did not work together. This was never clearer than in 1913 when Wells participated in the first women's suffrage march in Washington, D.C. White suffragist Alice Paul had just joined the National American Woman Suffrage Association (NAWSA). One of the first things she did as part of NAWSA was organize the parade. It was so controversial, newspapers from all over the country were there to cover it.

When the parade was about to start, Wells and the rest of the Alpha Suffrage Group lined up with other delegates from Illinois. Before the parade started, they were told they would have to march in the back—behind the white women. This, the organizers argued, would avoid upsetting the watching crowd, which was mostly white.

The Woman Suffrage Procession was the first civil rights parade in Washington, D.C. Women came from around the country to show the U.S. government how serious they were about getting the right to vote.

Inez Milholland led the Woman Suffrage Procession on horseback. A labor lawyer who worked for world peace and for equality for African Americans. Milholland was a member of the NAACP.

The order did not go over well with Wells. She was determined to march with the rest of the protesters from her state. She told them, "Either I go with you or not at all. I am not taking this stand because I personally wish for recognition. I am doing it for the future benefit of my whole race."[3] She then walked past the black women she'd brought with her, past the white women, and to the white men walking at the front. There, she marched where everyone could see her.

When she was 67 years old, Ida B. Wells-Barnett had become known for saying she was tired of the "do-nothings" in politics.[4] Thinking she could do better, in 1930 she did something few women before her had even dreamed of: she ran for office. When she did not succeed at joining the Illinois State Senate, she wrote a biography instead. In it, she wrote, "Our youth are entitled to the facts of race history, which only the participants can give." [5]

This would be her last piece of writing. On March 25, 1931, Ida B. Wells-Barnett died of kidney disease. Her words, and her message, lived on.

While she was very busy with her work, Wells-Barnett always made time for her children Charles, Herman, Ida, and Alfreda.

Checkout Receipt
Harris County Public Library
Renew your items online:
http://catalog.hcpl.net

Title: Ida B. Wells
Call Number: B Wellsb
Item ID: 34028100644773
Date Due: 3/4/2024

Title: Power In My Pen : A Snippet
Of The Life Of Id...
Call Number: B Wellsb
Item ID: 34028096308177
Date Due: 3/4/2024

Title: Who Was Ida B. Wells?
Call Number: B WellsB
Item ID: 34028103058088
Date Due: 3/4/2024

ALICE PAUL AND THE SILENT SENTINELS

Not long after the March on Washington in 1913, Alice Paul left NAWSA and started another group, the National Women's Party (NWP). On January 10, 1917, members of this group of women began holding a silent vigil outside the White House. They were upset that Woodrow Wilson still did not support women's suffrage. They held signs saying things like, "Mr President, what will you do for woman's suffrage?" and "Mr. President, how long must women wait for liberty?" The women were angry with President Wilson. He was fighting a World War overseas for freedom, and yet he would not give the women in his own country the freedom to vote.

The protest lasted more than two years and was completely silent. Even when they burned the president's speeches in a pot by the gate, they did not speak. These Silent Sentinels, with their Grand Sentinel Protest, refused to leave their corner. They protested every single day, all day, until June 1919, when Congress passed the amendment that allowed women to vote. A year later, on August 18, 1920, the amendment was ratified and became law.[6]

Silent Sentinels protest at the White House.

STILL RIGHTING WRONGS

CHAPTER FIVE

In her 68 years, Ida B. Wells-Barnett was many things. She was an activist who tried to change the quality of life for African Americans. She was a feminist deeply involved in women's suffrage. She was a mother to her siblings and then a mother to her own children. Even now, years after her death, Wells-Barnett continues to play a role.

One of the most significant symbols of Wells-Barnett is the Wells-Barnett House in Chicago. She and her husband bought the house in 1919 and remained there until 1929. Many of her most important efforts took place while she lived in this home. It is located at 3624 S. Martin Luther King Drive in Chicago. A National Historic Landmark, it is a private residence and does not allow visitors. This doesn't mean that tourists don't still look up at the house and smile at the fire of activism that once burned within it.

Wells-Barnett and her family lived in this home in Chicago from 1919 to 1929.

Children play in front of the Ida B. Wells Housing Project in 1973.

The Ida B. Wells Housing Project was opened in 1941. This was a place for African Americans to live and feel safe. This housing was later torn down, but the location stayed important to the people of Chicago for many years. In 2015, the Ida B. Wells Commemorative Art Committee began raising money to place a statue of Ida B. Wells-Barnett where the housing project used to stand. Daniel Duster, a great-grandson of Wells, said this about the planned location for the statue: "To be sitting here, where the housing development was, and to have that [sculpture] be the center piece. . . it gives me chills in a positive way to say that's the way she's going to be honored, and that's the way the community is going to be celebrated."[1]

The biggest acknowledgement of Wells-Barnett's contributions came in 1988 with the Ida B. Wells Memorial Foundation. Its purpose is "to protect, preserve, and promote the legacy of Ida B. Wells."[2] The foundation promotes lectures at churches, universities, museums, and to women's organizations all across the United States. In connection with the foundation is the Ida B. Wells Museum in Holly Springs, Mississippi. There, visitors can walk through the land originally owned by Spires Bolling and think of how far Wells came from her beginnings as a slave.

There is no better place to truly appreciate the journey of Wells' life than at her first home in Holly Springs, Massachusetts.

Ida B. Wells-Barnett once said, "The people must know before they can act, and there is no educator to compare with the press."[3] In 2015, four black reporters were deeply inspired by this civil rights activist. These reporters were Nikole Hannah-Jones, Ron Nixon, Corey Johnson, and Topher Sanders. There were few people of color in investigative reporting. Together, the four decided this needed to change, and that they would do it in the name of Ida B. Wells-Barnett. A society was created that offered the training and mentorship black people needed to succeed as investigative reporters. The society hosted their first meeting in Memphis, Tennessee. This was to honor Wells-Barnett, who had to flee from Memphis after releasing articles on lynching. In August 2016, the Ida B. Wells Society was officially launched.[4]

If Wells-Barnett were alive today, she would probably be thrilled about the progress the United States has made. There is no slavery on American soil. Women are allowed to vote. People of color are better represented in politics and all kinds of businesses. But improvements can still be made, and surely she would continue to fight for racial and gender equality.

No matter what the future brings, people who stand up for what's right, like Wells-Barnett, will always be needed. In her own words, "The way to right wrongs is to turn the light of truth upon them."[5]

Some famous people have big beginnings. Ida B. Wells was a famous person, a powerful woman, but she had a small beginning. She was an inspiration when she was alive and she is still an inspiration today.

BLACK LIVES MATTER

A lot of advances have been made in the civil rights movement since the time of Ida B. Wells-Barnett, but there is still a long way to go. One of the newer organizations to promote civil rights is Black Lives Matter.

In 2013, three African American women came together. Their names were Alicia Garza, Patrisse Cullors, and Opal Tometi. All three women had seen the hardship their fellow African Americans were experiencing. They wanted to change that, but how?

They began a local effort called Black Lives Matter. It might have started out small, but it soon became an international movement. It now has more than 40 chapters and is a political force.

Black Lives Matter has many goals. It protects and advocates for African American communities. It hosts protests and fights back against injustices such as police brutality. It also promotes change in the criminal justice system to bring equal treatment for those accused of crimes.

A Black Lives Matter supporter

1861	The Civil War begins.
1862	Ida B. Wells is born on July 16.
1865	The Emancipation Proclamation goes into effect. The Civil War ends.
1875	The Civil Rights Act of 1875 makes it illegal to segregate public places such as railroad cars and theaters.
1878	Yellow fever claims the lives of up to 20,000 people in the Mississippi Valley, including the parents and one sibling of Ida B. Wells.
Around 1880	Ida and two of her sisters move in with their aunt in Memphis, Tennessee. Ida begins teaching and taking classes to further her career.
1883	Wells refuses to change cars on a train. The Supreme Court rules that the Civil Rights Act of 1875 is unconstitutional.
1892	Thomas Moss, owner of the People's Grocery, is lynched.
1893	Black Americans are refused entry to World's Columbian Exposition (Chicago World's Fair).
1895	Wells marries Ferdinand Lee Barnett.
1896	She starts the National Association for Colored Women.
1898	Outside the White House, she protests lynching.
1908	She joins the National Association for the Advancement of Colored People (NAACP).
1910	She founds the Negro Fellowship League.

1913	Wells founds the Alpha Suffrage Group. She refuses to walk at the back of a women's suffrage march, instead marching with the white members of the Illinois delegation.
1917	On January 10, the Silent Sentinels begin their protest for women's suffrage outside the White House.
1920	The 19th Amendment is ratified, giving women the right to vote.
1931	Wells dies of kidney disease on March 25.
1941	The first residents move into the Ida B. Wells Homes in Chicago.
1955	Rosa Parks refuses to give up her seat on a bus in Montgomery, Alabama.
1964	President Lyndon B. Johnson signs the Civil Rights Act, which prohibits racial discrimination in employment and education, and outlaws segregation in public facilities.
1983	The National Association of Black Journalists begins The Ida B. Wells Award.
1988	The Ida B. Wells Memorial Foundation is formed.
1990	Ida B. Wells-Barnett appears on a U.S. postage stamp.
2011	The last of the Ida B. Wells Homes are torn down.
2016	The Ida B. Wells Society is launched.
2018	*The Ladies Car,* a play based on the life of Wells-Barnett, begins touring through the U.S.

Chapter One. Treating Her Like a Lady

1. Wells-Barnett, Ida B. "A Legal Brief for Ida B. Wells' Lawsuit Against Chesapeake, Ohio, and Southwestern Railroad Company Before the State Supreme Court, 1885." *Digital Public Library of America*. March 31, 1885. https://dp.la/primary-source-sets/ida-b-wells-and-anti-lynching-activism/sources/1113

2. History.com. "Rosa Parks." *History.com*. 2009. http://www.history.com/topics/black-history/rosa-parks

Chapter Two. Born into War

1. Black, Patti Carr. "Ida B. Wells: A Courageous Voice for Civil Rights." *Mississippi History Now*. Unknown date. http://www.mshistorynow.mdah.ms.gov/articles/49/ida-b-wells-a-courageous-voice-for-civil-rights

2. McBride, Jennifer. "Ida B. Wells: Crusade for Justice." *Women's Intellectual Contributions to Society*. http://faculty.webster.edu/woolflm/idabwells.html

Chapter Three. Losing Family, Losing Friends

1. McBride, Jennifer. "Ida B. Wells: Crusade for Justice." *Women's Intellectual Contributions to Society*. http://faculty.webster.edu/woolflm/idabwells.html

2. Ibid.

3. NAACP. "History of Lynchings." http://www.naacp.org/history-of-lynchings/

Chapter Four. The Princess of the Press

1. Truman, Margaret. *Women of Courage from Revolutionary Times to the Present*. New York: William Morrow and Co., 1976.

2. Rhoads, Mark. "Illinois Hall of Fame: Ida B. Wells." *Illinois Review*. November, 2006. http://illinoisreview.typepad.com/illinoisreview/2006/11/illinois_hall_o_29.html

3. Janigro, Alice. "Ida B. Wells." *Suffrage 100*. http://suffrage100ma.org/ida-b-wells/

4. Myrick-Harris, Clarissa. "Against All Odds." *Smithsonian*. June 30, 2002. https://www.smithsonianmag.com/arts-culture/against-all-odds-65322127/

5. Ibid.

6. Sun, Rivera. "Silent Sentinels Start Suffrage Protest on January 10th, 1917." *Rivera Sun*. January 8, 2016. http://www.riverasun.com/silent-sentinels-start-suffrage-protest-on-jan-10th-1917/

Chapter Five. Still Righting Wrongs

1. "Honoring Ida B. Wells with Chicago's First Monument to an African American Woman." *Business and Professional People for the Public Interest*. October 22, 2015. https://www.bpichicago.org/blog/honoring-ida-b-wells-with-chicagos-first-monument-to-an-african-american-woman/

2. "The Ida B. Wells Memorial Foundation." Unknown date. http://www.ibwfoundation.org/

3. Haouchine, Asiya. "Today in History: Ida B. Wells." *War Scapes*. July 16, 2015. http://www.warscapes.com/blog/today-history-ida-b-wells

4. *The Ida B. Wells Society*. "Our Creation Story." http://idabwellssociety.org/about/our-creation-story/

5. Edwards, Phil. "How Ida B. Wells Became a Trailblazing Journalist." *Vox*. July 16, 2015. https://www.vox.com/2015/7/16/8978257/ida-b-wells

Books

DK. *Eyewitness Books: Civil War*. London: DK Children, 2015.

Jazynka, Kitson. *National Geographic Readers: Rosa Parks*. Washington, D.C.: National Geographic Kids, August 2015.

McDonough, Yona Zeldis. *Who Was Rosa Parks?* London, England: Penguin Workshop, 2010.

Meltzer, Brand. *I Am Martin Luther King, Jr.* London, England: Dial Books, 2016.

Myers, Walter Dean. *Ida B. Wells: Let the Truth Be Told*. New York: Amistad, 2015.

Wilson, Janet. *Our Rights: How Kids Are Changing the World*. Toronto, Canada: Second Story Press, 2013.

Works Consulted

Bay, Mia. *To Tell the Truth Freely: The Life of Ida B. Wells*. New York: Hill and Wang, 2010.

Benz, Robert J. "Ida B. Wells' Old Advice for the NAACP's 'New Direction.'" *Huffpost*. May 22, 2017. https://www.huffingtonpost.com/entry/ida-b-wells-old-advice-for-the-naacps-new-direction_us_591fa439e4b07617ae4cbc2d

Black, Patti Carr. "Ida B. Wells: A Courageous Voice for Civil Rights." *Mississippi History Now*. February 2001. http://www.mshistorynow.mdah.ms.gov/articles/49/ida-b-wells-a-courageous-voice-for-civil-rights

Duster, A. (Ed.). *Crusade for Justice: The Autobiography of Ida B. Wells*. Chicago: University of Chicago Press, 1970.

Giddings, Paula J. *Ida: A Sword Among Lions*. New York: Harper Paperbacks, 2009.

Riley, Ricky. "10 Facts You May Not Have Known About Ida B. Wells." *Atlanta Black Star*. July 16, 2014. http://atlantablackstar.com/2014/07/16/10-facts-may-known-ida-b-wells/

On the Internet

Ida B. Wells Memorial Foundation
   http://www.ibwfoundation.org/

Ida B. Wells Society
   http://idabwellssociety.org/

Children play outside homes that Ida B. Wells helped create.

activist (AK-tih-vist)—A person who tries to bring about political or social change.

amendment (ah-MEND-ment)—An official change to the U.S. Constitution.

bondage (BON-dij)—The situation of belonging to another person as a slave.

carpenter (KAR-pen-ter)—A person who makes or repairs wooden objects.

conductor (kun-DUK-ter)—The person in charge of a train and who checks tickets on board.

discrimination (dis-krim-ih-NAY-shun)—The unfair treatment of someone based on their race, gender, religion, or ability.

embellish (em-BEL-ish)—To add details, even untrue details, to a story to make it more interesting.

feminist (FEH-mih-nist)—Someone who supports equal rights for women.

liberty (LIH-ber-tee)—The freedom to think and behave freely.

lynch (LINCH)—To kill someone, usually by hanging, even though they have not been proved guilty of a crime.

Negro (NIH-groh)—A black person (outdated term).

racism (RAY-sism)—The unfair treatment of a person based on their race.

ratify (RAT-ih-fy)—For an ammendment, to gain enough support from the states to pass.

segregation (seh-greh-GAY-shun)—Separating people based on race.

sue (SOO)—To take another person to court over a legal conflict.

A sign in Memphis, Tennessee celebrating the legacy of Ida B. Wells

suffrage (SUH-fridj)—The right to vote.

understatement (UN-der-stayt-ment)—A description of something that makes it seem smaller or less important than it actually is.

yellow fever (YEH-loh FEE-ver)—A deadly disease that causes a high fever and the skin to turn yellow; it is carried by mosquitoes.

PHOTO CREDITS: P. 5—Rail Relics Today; pp. 7, 14, 31—Loc.gov; p. 13—Golbez, TorninTwo2011; p. 21—Thomas R. Machnitzki; p. 23—Global Panorama; p. 25—Mary Garrity; p. 35—Tonythetiger. All other photos—Public Domain. Every measure has been taken to find all copyright holders of material used in this book. In the event any mistakes or omissions have happened within, attempts to correct them will be made in future editions of the book.